To:

Copyright © 1995
Peter Pauper Press, Inc.
202 Mamaroneck Avenue
White Plains, NY 10601
All rights reserved
ISBN 0-88088-932-2
Printed in China
7   6   5   4   3   2

The Language of Flowers

Solomon M. Skolnick

Design by
Mullen & Katz

PETER PAUPER PRESS, INC.
WHITE PLAINS, NEW YORK

INTRODUCTION

*O*ur fondness for symbols—the use of objects
to remind us of an event or represent a sentiment or
emotion—has seldom found a more beautiful palette
than in the floral world. The Near Eastern tradition
of creating messages without words, without sounds,
using various objects, found its transfer point into
France and later England at the beginning of the
19th century. Once in Europe, this symbol language
was fashioned to take advantage of a budding interest
in unusual and exotic plants.

Charlotte de la Tour's *Le langage des fleurs*,
published in 1819, was a huge popular success.
Translated into a myriad of languages, it led the way
for Elizabeth Kent's 1823 *Flora
Domestica*, the first English-origi-
nated floral interpreter. Dozens of
works such as *Flora Symbolica*,
Flora's Lexicon, *The Poetry of*

[5]

Flowers, Phillips Floral Emblems and *The Language and Sentiment of Flowers* followed. The increased access to a large vocabulary of floral meanings popularized by these books encouraged this esthetically pleasing method of communicating subtle messages between men and women. In addition to the basic sentiment assigned to a particular flower, the color and position of the elements of a bouquet clarified, sometimes to the dismay, sometimes to the delight of the recipient, the true meaning of the message.

We have inherited a rich floral heritage that provides sensual delight for the eyes, the nose, and the tips of the fingers. Even if you are not about to sit down and create a tussie-mussie ("a nosegay with a message"), the phrases, meanings, and illustrations in this modern potpourri of flora's language will most certainly bring you joy.

The Language of Flowers

An exquisite invention this,

Worthy of Love's most honeyed kiss, —

This art of writing billet-doux

In buds and flowers and bright hues!

In saying all one feels and thinks

In clever daffodils and pinks;

In puns of tulips, and in phrases,

Charming for their truth of daisies!

James Henry Leigh-Hunt

ACACIA
Friendship deep, a love so chaste

ACACIA, PINK
Elegance in bloom

ACACIA, YELLOW
Signals a secret love whose name dies upon the lips.

ALMOND
One that does not flower holds the seed of
indiscretion.

ALMOND, FLOWERING
Portends the blossoming
of hope

ALOE
Bitterness, grief, sorrow; how unfair to a plant that
holds the power to heal

ALYSSUM
Sweetness of soul and countenance; an attribute
valued beyond the worth of transitory beauty

AMARANTH
Immortality

AMARANTH, GLOBE
Unchangeable, incorruptible; love
that does not fade in the sharp
light of day or with the cares and
temptations of time

The Language of Flowers

The infinite has written its name
on the heavens in shining stars,
and on the earth in tender flowers.

Jean Paul Richter

AMARYLLIS
A fiery show of pride illuminating splendid,
but short-lived, beauty

AMBROSIA
Sweet love returned

ANEMONE
(WINDFLOWER)
Love abandoned now dispersed
on the wind

APPLE
Temptation, Eve's or anyone else's

ARBORVITAE
Enduring friendship

ASTER
Variety, elegance, daintiness, patience

AZALEA
Temperance

BACHELOR'S BUTTONS
A singular joy!

BAY WREATH
Glory, reward of merit

BEGONIA
Dark thoughts or attention

BERGAMOT (BEE BALM)
Sympathy and consolation

BORAGE
Blunt and brusque. Diplomacy does
not bloom here.

BUTTERCUP
Ingratitude, childishness

*I find the children of the garden
more consistent in their behavior than
the children of men; they have not
unlearned the great law of obedience.
Each individual and family and tribe
has its standard and rule of conduct
and lives by it, and when we grow
we recognize it, we have the peace
which comes from our confidence in the
behavior of a tried friend.*

Candace Wheeler

BUTTERFLY FLOWER
Gaiety

BUTTERFLY WEED
(MILKWEED)
Let me go, our paths do part,
and we're both the better for it!

CAMELLIA JAPONICA, WHITE
Loveliness perfected, like the flower itself

CAMOMILE
The ability to battle adversity with
energy and conviction

CAMPANULA BELLFLOWER
Gratitude

CAMPANULA BLUEBELL
Constancy

CAMPANULA HAREBELL
Grief

CANDY TUFT
The chill of indifference

CARNATION, RED
This poor heart has suffered more than its
share of misfortune.

Just after the death of the flowers,

And before they are buried in snow,

There comes a festival season

When nature is all aglow.

❧

Anonymous

CARNATION, STRIPED
Refusal

CELANDINE
The joys to come will more than
reward the unpleasantness that
is here now.

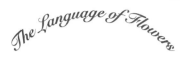
CHINA ASTER, DOUBLE
Your sentiments are mine.

CHINA ASTER, SINGLE
I will think about it and let you know
if I share your point of view.

CHRISTMAS ROSE (HELLEBORE)
Relieve me of my anxious thoughts.
A word or two will do.

CHRYSANTHEMUM, RED
I love.

CHRYSANTHEMUM, WHITE
Truth comes easily,
lies require imagination.

I used to love my garden,
But now my love is dead,
For I found a bachelor's button
In black-eyed Susan's bed.

❧

Anonymous

CLEMATIS
A beautiful mind creates objects of beauty.

CLOVER, FOUR-LEAVED
Be mine. You are lucky. The recipients are even
luckier if they respond to the first meaning with
Ambrosia—sweet love returned.

CLOVER, WHITE
Think of me.

COLUMBINE
Folly

COLUMBINE, PURPLE
Resolved and steadfast

COLUMBINE, RED
Anxious and trembling; I don't know what to expect.

COREOPSIS
Always cheerful, ever bright

COWSLIP, AMERICAN
You are my angel.

CROCUS, SPRING FLOWERING
The joys and feelings of youth are yours
no matter what your age may be.

CYPRESS
Mourning

DAFFODIL
Regard

DAFFODIL, GREAT YELLOW
Chivalry; in an earlier time called the chalice flower.

DAHLIA, SINGLE
Good taste is rewarded with admiring glances.

DAISY, MICHAELMAS
Farewell

DAISY, PARTI-COLORED
Beauty

DAISY, WHITE
Innocence

A solitary maple on a woodside
flames in single scarlet, recalls nothing
so much as the daughter of a noble house
dressed for a fancy ball, with the whole
family gathered round to admire her
before she goes.

Henry James

D A I S Y ,   W I L D
I will think of what you have said,
and remember the sentiment
with fondness.

DANDELION
Oracle of love

The Dandelion
With locks of gold today;
Tomorrow silver gray;
Then blossom—bald. Behold,
O man, thy fortune told!

John Banister Tabb

DELPHINIUM
Well being, heavenly

DIANTHUS
A mother's love

DOGWOOD
(CORNELIAN CHERRY)
Love undiminished by hardship

E GLANTINE
(S WEET - B RIAR R OSE)
Poetry flows from the pen
of those who take this flower
as their own emblem.

E LM
Dignity

E VENING P RIMROSE
Inconstancy

FENNEL
Worthy of the praise that you receive

FERN
Sincerity

FERN, FLOWERING
Fascination with the spirits of the night

FIG
In conflict

FIG TREE
Prolific

FORGET ME NOT
True love

What is lovely never dies
But passes into other loveliness,
Star-dust, or sea-foam, flower,
or winged air

⚜

Thomas Bailey Aldrich

F O X G L O V E
Insincere

F R A X I N E L L A
Fire

GENTIAN
You are unjust.

GERANIUM, LEMON-SCENTED
A serendipitous meeting

GERANIUM, NUTMEG-SCENTED
A planned meeting

GERANIUM, ROSE-SCENTED
Preference

GERANIUM, SCARLET
Comforting

GERANIUM, WILD
Steadfast in piety

GILLYFLOWER
Lasting beauty; bound to each other
with deep affection

GLADIOLUS
Strong in character

GLOXINIA
A proud spirit

GOLDENROD
Caution.
Tread slowly and lightly.

GRASS
Useful

HAREBELL
Grieving

HAWTHORNE
Hope

HEATH
Solitude

HEATHER
Beauty in solitude

HELLEBORE
Scandal

HELIOTROPE
Intoxicated with pleasure

There is much of life in autumn. . . .
No leaf has dropped until a bud was born to it. . . .
The green heart-shaped leaves of the violet
tell me that all is well at the root; and in turning
the soil I find those spring beauties that died, to be
only sleeping. Heart, take courage. . . .
There is resurrection—hope not alone
in the garden . . . Every flower and every tree and
every root are annual prophets sent to affirm the
future and cheer the way.

❦

Henry Ward Beecher

HEPATICA
Confidence

HIBISCUS
A most delicate beauty

HOLLY
Foresight

HOLLYHOCK
Ambitious, fecund, fruitful

HONEYSUCKLE
Generous with affection and a most devoted friend

HYACINTH, PURPLE
Constant companion, constant source of
pleasure and joy

If of thy mortal goods
thou art bereft,
And from thy slender store two loaves
alone to thee are left,
Sell one, and with the dole
Buy hyacinths to feed thy soul.

Saadi

HYACINTH, BLUE
Sorrow

HYACINTH, WHITE
Subtle loveliness

HYDRANGEA
A cold and uncaring spirit

ICE PLANT
Your looks leave me cold.

IMPATIENS (BALSAM)
Impatience

IRIS, BLUE
Herein lies the message.

IRIS, RED
I burn with passion's flame.

IRIS, YELLOW
The object of passion

IVY
The fidelity of marriage vows
held sacred

JACOB'S LADDER
Come down, relinquish your lofty airs.

JASMINE, WHITE
Amiable

JASMINE, CAPE
Bearer of joyous news

*Flowers and fruits are
always fit presents—flowers,
because they are a proud assertion that
a ray of beauty outvalues all the
utilities of the world.*

Ralph Waldo Emerson

JASMINE, CAROLINA
Separation

JASMINE, SPANISH
Sensuality

JASMINE, YELLOW
Graceful and elegant

JONQUIL
I wish that you would
return my affection in kind.

JUNIPER
Protection

LABURNUM
Forsaken

LADY'S MANTLE
The comfort of protection

LADY'S SLIPPER
Capricious

LANTANA
Rigorous and sharp

LARKSPUR
The lightness of spirit brought
about by laughter

LARKSPUR, PINK
Fickle charms are not a foundation
for friendship or love.

LAUREL
Glory

LAUREL, MOUNTAIN
Ambition

LAVENDER
Distrust of your motives

LILAC, PURPLE
First warm stirrings of love

LILAC, WHITE
Youthful innocence

LILY, IMPERIAL
Majesty

Consider the lilies of the field, how they grow;
they toil not, neither do they spin:
And yet I say unto you, That even Solomon in
all his glory was not arrayed like one of these.
Wherefore, if God so clothe the grass of the field,
which today is, and tomorrow is cast into the oven,
shall He not much more clothe you,
O ye of little faith?

Matthew 6:28-30 (KJV)

LILY, WHITE
Purity

LILY, YELLOW
Gaiety

LILY OF THE VALLEY
Return of happiness

LINDEN TREE
Will you marry me?

LOBELIA, SCARLET
Malevolence; spewing of
spiteful and angry remarks

LOTUS
A protective silence

LOTUS FLOWER
Estranged from a lover

LOTUS LEAF
Recantation

LUPINE
Imagination

MAGNOLIA
Love of nature

Nature chose for a tool,
not the earthquake or lightning to rend
and split asunder, not the stormy torrent
or eroding rain, but the tender
snow-flowers noiselessly falling through
unnumbered centuries. . . .

John Muir

MALLOW
Blessed with a sweet disposition

MALLOW, SYRIAN
Consumed by the passions and pleasures of love

MALLOW, VENETIAN
A fine and delicate beauty

MAPLE TREE
Reserved; shy and retiring

MARIGOLD
Despair

MARIGOLD, AFRICAN
They who are possessed of vulgar and
insensitive minds

MARIGOLD, FRENCH
Jealousy

MEADOWSWEET
Not of much use to anyone

MILK VETCH
I feel better when you are here.

MIMOSA
A sensitive soul

*I have here only made a
nosegay of culled flowers,
and have brought nothing of my own
but the thread that
ties them together.*

Michel de Montaigne

MINT
Virtue

MISTLETOE
Nothing to do with
holiday kisses; I overcome
difficult situations.

MOCK ORANGE
Counterfeit

MORNING GLORY
Sustained by affection

MOSS
Boredom

MUGWORT
Do not weary on your travels.

MYRTLE
Be my love and share the
peacefulness of my home.

NARCISSUS
Egotism, self-love

**NASTURTIUM,
SCARLET**
Splendor

NETTLE
Slander

NIGHTSHADE
False and dark thoughts

OAK LEAVES
Bravery

OAK TREE
Hospitality

OAK, WHITE
Independent spirit

OLEANDER
Be wary and on your guard.

OLIVE BRANCH
An offering of peace

ORANGE BLOSSOM
Chastity

ORANGE TREE
Generosity

ORCHID
A belle

To the Orchid:

Who hung thy beauty on such slender stalk,

Thou glorious flower?

Lydia Huntley Sigourney

PANSY
Think happy thoughts when you think of me.

PARSLEY
A feast or banquet

PASQUEFLOWER
You have no claim to pretension.

PASSIONFLOWER
Religious rite

PEA, SWEET
Departure

PEACH
Your qualities and charms are
without equal.

PEACH BLOSSOM
My heart is captive to you.

PEAR
Affection

PEAR TREE
Comfort

PEONY
Bashful

PERIWINKLE, BLUE
Budding friendship

Still—

in a way—

nobody sees a flower—

really—

it is so small—

we haven't time—

and to see takes time,

like to have a friend

takes time.

Georgia O'Keeffe

PERIWINKLE, WHITE
Pleasurable memories

PHLOX
Unanimity

PINE

Warm friendship

PINE TREE

Bold and daring

PINEAPPLE

Welcome to our home

PINK

Lively and pure affection

The Language of Flowers

PINK, CARNATION
The love of a woman

PINK, INDIAN DOUBLE
You will always be lovely.

PINK, MOUNTAIN
Aspiring

PINK, RED DOUBLE
Ardent love

PINK, SINGLE
Pure love expressed without condition

PINK, VARIEGATED
You are fair and fascinate me.

PLUM TREE
Fidelity

POLYANTHUS
(PRIMULA),
CRIMSON
The mysteries of the heart

POLYANTHUS
(PRIMULA),
LILAC
Confident

POPPY, RED
Consolation

POPPY, SCARLET
Fantastic extravagance

The Language of Flowers

The Decision of The Flower

And with scarlet poppies around, like a bower,

The maiden found her mystic flower;

"Now gentle flower, I pray thee tell

If my lover loves me, and loves me well;

So may the fall of the morning dew

Keep the sun from fading thy tender blue.

Now I number the leaves for my lot –

He loves me not – he loves me – he loves me not –

He loves me, – yes, thou last leaf, yes –

I'll pluck thee not for that last sweet guess!

He loves me!" – "Yes," a dear voice sigh'd,

And her lover stands
by Margaret's side.

Miss Landon,
from Flora's Lexicon

POPPY, WHITE
Adrift in a peaceful sleep

PRIMROSE
Youth

PRIVET
Prohibited

PUSSY WILLOW
Easter

QUAKING OATS
Entranced by the music

QUAMOCLIT (AMERICAN JASMINE)
Minding everybody's business but one's own

QUEEN'S ROCKET
She is always fashionable.

QUINCE
Temptation

RANUNCULUS
You are radiant with charm.

RANUNCULUS, GARDEN
You are attractive.

RANUNCULUS, WILD
Ungrateful

RASPBERRY
Remorse

REED, SINGLE
Complacent

REED, SPLIT
You have been indiscreet.

REEDS
Lured by a song

RHODODENDRON
In this path lies danger.

ROSE, AUSTRIAN
You embody all that is lovely.

ROSE, BURGUNDY
That which is simple is often most beautiful.

ROSE, CAMPION
Deserving of my love

ROSE, CAROLINA
Love despite its pleasures and its dangers

ROSE, CHINA
Graceful

ROSE, CHRISTMAS
You can make me feel
less anxious.

ROSE, FADED
Even the most vivid beauty is fleeting.

ROSE, GLOIRE DE DIJON
Messenger of love

*It is not the least of the tokens of the royalty
and dominion of the rose, that the choicest of sensa-
tions which we call color is called by its name.
We use it to describe a sunset sky or the tinting of a
baby's finger-tips; and even the innumerable
variations of shades and dyes of damasks and velvet
and precious silken stuffs which commend their tints
to human eyes, rose-colored describes, and the flower
mingles its remembrance with the
loveliest of them all.*

Candace Wheeler

ROSE, LA FRANCE
Meet me by moonlight.

ROSE, MAIDEN BLUSH
If you love me you will know.

ROSE, PROVENCE
My heart is warm with love.

ROSE, SINGLE
Simply stated

ROSE, THORNLESS
Love at first sight

ROSE, WHITE
I am worthy of you.

ROSE, WHITE
(WITHERED)
My feelings for you are
in transition.

ROSE,
WHITE AND RED TOGETHER
Unity

ROSE, YELLOW
Jealousy

ROSEBUD, RED
Pure and lovely

*The rose has almost a monopoly of admiration.
In love and literature, ancient and modern, it is a
leading figure. A mysterious something in
its nature, — an inner fascination,
a subtle witchery, a hidden charm which it
has . . . ensnares and holds
the love of the world.*

❀

Candace Wheeler

R O S E M A R Y
Remembrance

R U D B E C K I A
Justice

R U S H
Docile

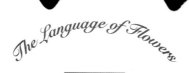

SAFFRON
Be honest with yourself.

SAFFRON, CROCUS
Joy and laughter

SAFFRON, MEADOW
I have good memories of
happy days gone by.

SAGE
A long and healthy life

SALVIA, BLUE
I am thinking of you.

SALVIA, RED
Energy and gusto

SAVORY
The truth may be bitter
but you must take it as it comes.

SNAPDRAGON
Presumptuous

SNOWDROP
Consoled by a friend
through adversity

SPIDERWORT
Held in esteem

STAR OF
BETHLEHEM
Purity

STONECROP
Tranquility

Flower in the crannied wall,

I pluck you out of the crannies,

I hold you here, root and all, in my hand,

Little flower—but if I could understand

What you are, root and all, and all in all,

I should know what God

and man is.

Alfred, Lord Tennyson

STRAWFLOWER
Always well remembered

SUNFLOWER
False riches

SUNFLOWER, DWARF
I adore you.

SUNFLOWER, TALL
Lofty and pure thoughts

SWEET BASIL
All good wishes

SWEET PEA
Delicate pleasures

SWEET WILLIAM
Accomplished with finesse

SYCAMORE
Curiosity

SYRINGA
A memory

TANSY
Resist what you do not truly desire.

THISTLE
Austere

THORN APPLE
Charmed by deception

THYME
Thrifty and active

THYME, NUTMEG
Sincerely devoted

THYME, SILVER-LEAF
A cherished memory of our
happiness together

TRUMPET FLOWER
Separation

TULIP, RED
I love you.

TULIP, VARIEGATED
Your eyes are beautiful.

TULIP, YELLOW
Unrequited love

VENUS
LOOKING-GLASS
Flattery

VERBENA
Enchantment

VERBENA, PINK
Strength in family

VERBENA, WHITE
Include me in your prayers.

VIOLET, BLUE
Faithful and loyal

VIOLET, WHITE
Modesty

WALLFLOWER
Faithful even in times of misfortune

WALNUT, BLACK
Intellect

WEEPING WILLOW
The melancholy of
a forsaken lover

WITCH HAZEL
Under a spell

WOOD HYACINTH
Delicate and alone

WOOD SORREL
Unencumbered joy

WOODBINE
Love for a brother or sister

WOODRUFF, SWEET
Of modest value

XANTHIUM
Rudeness

YEW
Sorrow

ZINNIA
Thoughts of absent friends

The Zinnia's solitary flower,

Which blooms in forests lone and deep,

Are like the visions fair and bright,

That faithful, absent hearts will keep.

Flora's Interpreter

The End